P9-CDI-449

a gift for:
from:

Published by Gift Books from Hallmark, a division of Hallmark Cards, Inc., Kansas City, MO 64141
Visit us on the Web at www.Hallmark.com.

Art Director: Kevin Swanson
Editorial Director: Todd Hafer
Illustration by: Cary Phillips
Designed by: Michelle Nicolier
Production Artist: Dan Horton

Editorial development by Scott Degelman & Associates, with additional writing by Trieste Van Wyngarden

BOK2073
ISBN 10: 1-59530-138-0
ISBN 13: 978-1-59530-138-3
Printed and bound in China

OLD AGE ain't no place for sissies

Old age is no place for sissies.

Bette Davis

Here's something that we'll all do today, regardless of our social status, ethnic background, or political party: We'll get older. Sure, some people handle it better than others, but it happens to all of us.

We all watch our skin migrating south like a flock of eager geese, our hairs fading to pale imitations of what they once were, our joints creaking like old rocking chairs.
That's just life.

Aging, though, has its benefits. Wisdom comes with age (if we can remember what we were talking about).

We become role models for the younger generations (if they can see past our uncool clothes).

We become respected, admired members of society. (Or at least we've been around long enough to avoid obsessing about what society thinks.)

This book is a celebration of the inevitable – and a tribute to the bold souls who refuse to take growing older lying down. (Sitting down works just as well.) So pull up a recliner, grab the bifocals, and enjoy a fresh look at an "old" topic.

Words *from the* Witty,
the Wise, the Weathered

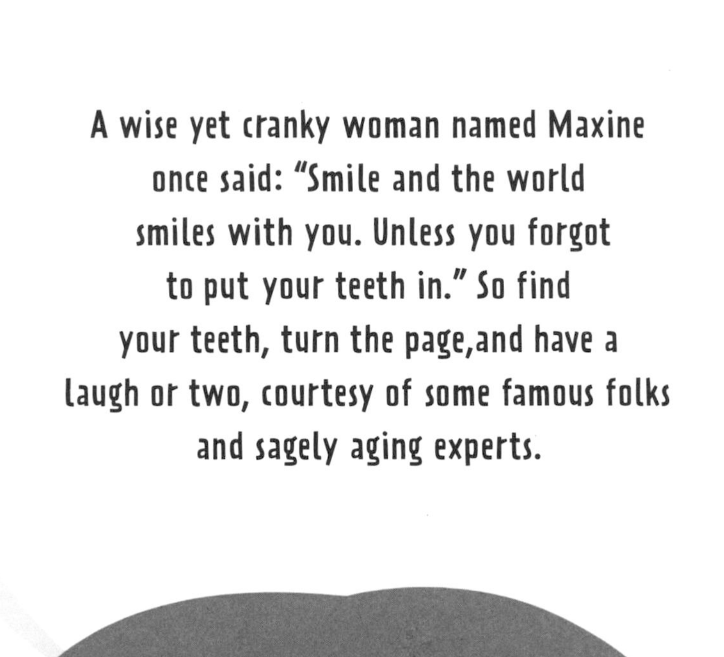

A wise yet cranky woman named Maxine
once said: "Smile and the world
smiles with you. Unless you forgot
to put your teeth in." So find
your teeth, turn the page,and have a
laugh or two, courtesy of some famous folks
and sagely aging experts.

Age is a question of mind over matter.
If you don't mind, it doesn't matter.

– Satchel Paige

Fortunate are those
who actually enjoy old age.

– Jewish Proverb

It takes one a long time to become young.

– Pablo Picasso

Life would be infinitely happier if only we could be born at the age of 80 and gradually approach 18.

– Mark Twain

You can't help getting older,
but you don't have to get old.

– George Burns

I am a man still in process.

– Billy Graham

If you carry your childhood with you,
you never become older.

– Abraham Sutzkever

I don't let old age bother me.
There are three signs of old age.
Loss of memory . . . I forget the other two.

– Red Skelton

"Don't worry about senility,"
my grandfather used to say.
"When it hits you, you won't know it."

– Bill Cosby

If wrinkles must be written
upon our brows,
let them not be written upon the heart.
The spirit should *never grow old.*

– James A. Garfield

Wrinkles should merely indicate
where smiles have been.

– Mark Twain

Forever
Young
Power
LiFT
WRINKLE
B
GONE
Magic
Miracle

Whatever wrinkles I got,
I enjoyed getting them.

– Ava Gardner

Outwardly I am 83, but inwardly I am every age,
with the emotions and experience of each period.

– Elizabeth Coatsworth

Retirement at 65 is ridiculous.
When I was 65, I still had pimples.

– George Burns

If I had known I would live this long,
I would have taken better care of myself.

– H. J. Springston (age 77)

At my age, by the time I find temptation,
I'm too tired to give in to it.

– E. C. McKenzie

The great comfort of turning 49 is the realization
that you are now too old to die young.

– Paul Dickson

Middle age:
When you begin to
exchange your emotions
for symptoms.

– Irvin Cobb

At fifty, everyone has the face he deserves.

– George Orwell

The problem with hitting 50 is that 50 hits back.

– Cheryl Hawkinson

To me, old age is always fifteen years older than I am.

– Bernard Baruch

Middle age is when your age
starts to show around your middle.

–Bob Hope

Retirement must be wonderful. I mean,
you can suck in your stomach for only so long.

– Burt Reynolds

As you get older,

the pickings

get slimmer,

but the people don't.

– Carrie Fisher

Women are just beginning at forty.
At fifty, you hit your power.

– Lauren Hutton

The man who views the world at 50 the same
as he did at 20 has wasted 30 years of his life.

– Muhammad Ali

Once you get past the fear of being responsible,
it feels good. At forty, it suddenly seems unattractive
to be a boy and very attractive to be a man.

– Paul Simon

Almost all enduring success comes to people after they are 40. For seldom does mature judgment arrive before then.

– Henry Ford

It is so comic to hear oneself called old, even at ninety I suppose!

– Alice James

There are years that ask questions and years that answer.

– Zora Neale Hurston

Man is old when he begins to hide his age;
woman, when she begins to tell hers.

– Oscar Wilde

You're not too old until it takes
longer to rest up than it does to get tired.

– Phog Allen

Careful grooming may take twenty years off
a woman's age, but you can't fool a long flight of stairs.

– Marlene Dietrich

Perhaps one has to be very old before one learns how to *be amused* rather than shocked.

– Pearl S. Buck

A man is not old until regrets take the place of *dreams*.

– John Barrymore

I am not *young enough* to know everything.

– Oscar Wilde

Anyone who stops learning is old,
whether at twenty or eighty.
Anyone who keeps learning stays young.

—Henry Ford

It's funny how you can go through life
thinking you've seen everything...
then you suddenly realize there are millions
of things you've never seen before.

– Charles Schulz

Every man's memory is his private literature.

– Aldous Huxley

Constant use will not wear ragged
the fabric of friendship.

– Dorothy Parker

You know you're getting old
when the candles cost more than the cake.

– Bob Hope

We need old friends
to help us grow old
and new friends
to help us stay young.

– Letty Cottin Pogrebin

Like a lot of the fellows out here, I have a furniture problem. My chest has fallen into my drawers.

– Billy Casper

You know you're getting old when you stoop to tie your shoes and wonder what else you can do while you're down there.

– George Burns

I have everything now that I had twenty years ago, except now it's all lower.

– Gypsy Rose Lee

I *love* everything that's old –
old friends, old times, old manners, old books, old wine.

– Oliver Goldsmith

I was hoping to be on *easy street*
by now, but I missed
the off-ramp years ago.

– Ed Wallerstein

Old age isn't *so bad* when you consider the alternative.

– Maurice Chevalier

There are only three ages for women in Hollywood – Babe, District Attorney, and Driving Miss Daisy.

–Goldie Hawn

A diplomat is a man who always remembers his wife's birthday but never remembers her age.

– Robert Frost

There are only two things a child will share willingly – communicable diseases and his mother's age.

– Dr. Benjamin Spock

Fun is like insurance: the older you get,
the more it costs.

–Elbert Hubbard

I never think of the future. It comes soon enough.

–Albert Einstein

To see a young couple loving each other
is no wonder, but to see
an old couple loving each other is the best sight of all.

– William Makepeace Thackeray

So much has been said and sung
of the beautiful young girls.
Why don't somebody wake up
to the beauty of old women?

– Harriet Beecher Stowe

Older women are best
because they always think
they may be doing it for the last time.

– Ian Fleming

Learning and sex until rigor mortis.

– Maggie Kuhn

The young man knows the rules,
but the old man knows the exceptions.

– Oliver Wendell Holmes

I am long on ideas, but short on time.
I expect to live to be only about 100.

– Thomas Edison (who lived to be 84)

Gray hair is God's graffiti.

—Bill Cosby

You're the only one who is passionately
interested in your age;
other people have their own troubles.

– Dorothy Parker

I will never give in to old age until I become old.
And I'm not old yet!

—Tina Turner

The secret of staying young
is to live honestly,
eat slowly,
and lie about your age.

– Lucille Ball

I don't worry about getting old. I'm old already.
Only young people worry about getting old.

– George Burns

Cherish all your happy moments;
they make a fine cushion for old age.

– Booth Tarkington

If you pull out a gray hair, seven will come to its funeral.

– German proverb

Inside every older person is a younger person – wondering what the hell happened.

– Cora Harvey Armstrong

There is no cure for birth and death, save to enjoy the interval.

– George Santayana

The great thing about getting older is that you don't lose all the other ages you've been.

– Madeleine L'Engle

Old people who
shine from the inside look
10 to 20 years younger.

– Dolly Parton

I'm saving that rocker for the day
when I feel as old as I really am.

– Dwight Eisenhower

But though an old man, I am but a young gardener.

– Thomas Jefferson

When I grow up, I want to be a little boy.

– Joseph Heller

We get too soon old, and too late smart.

– German proverb

She was so old that when she went to school,
they didn't have history.

– Rodney Dangerfield

I intend to remain young indefinitely.

– Mary Pickford

When I was young, the Dead Sea was alive.

– George Burns

I look forward to growing old and wise and audacious.

–Glenda Jackson

In love, as in other matters,
the young are just beginners.

– Isaac Bashevis Singer

Youth is a gift of nature, but age is a work of art.

– Garson Kanin

It's great getting old.

– Harrison Ford

One should never trust a woman
who tells one her real age.
A woman who would tell that would tell anything.

– Oscar Wilde

What I look forward to
is continued *immaturity*, followed by death.

– Dave Barry

The young man who has not wept is a savage,
and the old man who will not laugh is a fool.

– George Santayana

Old minds are like old horses:
you must exercise them if you
wish to keep them in working order.

– John Quincy Adams

The man who is too old to learn
was probably always too old to learn.

–Henry S. Haskins

When you get old, you might lose some
of your marbles. But don't lose your marvels.

– Taylor Morgan

Age doesn't matter, unless you're a cheese.

– J. Paul Getty

Aging like a fine wine
means spending a lot
of time on your side, lying down.

– Kevin Kinzer

Beauty comes in all ages, colors, shapes, and forms. God never makes junk.

– Kathy Ireland

Too many people grow up. That's the real trouble with the world. . . . They don't remember what it's like to be twelve years old.

– Walt Disney

It's better to *wear out* than to rust out.

– Mary Miró

It's not how old you are, *but* how you are old.

–Marie Dressler

PROPERTY OF
STAN'S
GYM

I never look back...
I'm not going that way.

– Ginnie Job

If we should live a thousand years,
our time is all today, today.

– James Montgomery

Surely the consolation
of old age is finding out
how few things
are worth worrying over.

– Dorothy Dix

To yackety-yak about the past is,
for me, time lost. Every morning,
I wake up saying, "I'm still alive – a miracle."
And so I keep on pushing.

– Jacques Cousteau

Youth is almost everything else,
but it is hardly ever original.

– G. K. Chesterton

When I stand before God at the end of my life,
I would hope that I would not have a single
bit of talent left and could say:
"I *used everything* You gave me."

– Erma Bombeck

If your experiences would benefit anybody,
give them to someone.

– Florence Nightingale

50 Things You Have Permission to Do (or Not Do) Now That You're Officially Old

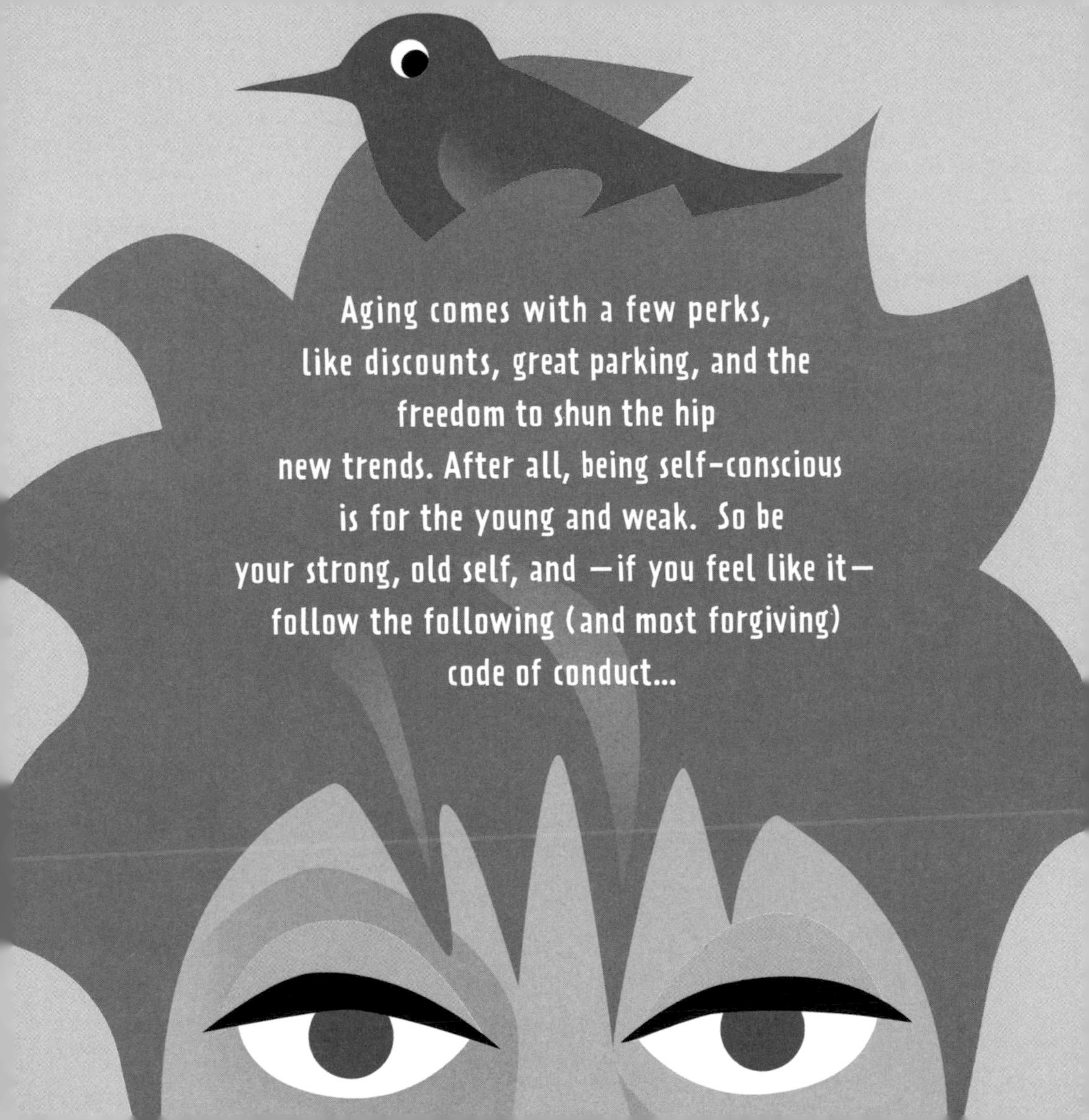

Aging comes with a few perks,
like discounts, great parking, and the
freedom to shun the hip
new trends. After all, being self-conscious
is for the young and weak. So be
your strong, old self, and —if you feel like it—
follow the following (and most forgiving)
code of conduct...

1. Say what you believe – out loud – even if it's outrageous.

2. Hit somebody in the back with a snowball; you'll be the last person anyone will suspect.

3. Don't worry about avoiding temptation; at your age, you'll find that temptation will do a fine job of avoiding you.

4. *Wear* the comfortable clothes . . .
same with the shoes.

5. *Go ahead* and eat food with lots
of preservatives in them—
all those preservatives
might work on you!

6. **Spend more time dreaming, hoping and planning– and less time regretting.**

7. Take up a new hobby –
or resume an old favorite.
Remember, the paintbrush, tennis racket,
or pen doesn't know, or care, how old you are.

8. Don't be afraid to pack your life
with lots of activities and interests.
Remember, you're over the hill;
it's OK to pick up speed.

9. Listen to the music you *want* to listen to. *Don't worry* about what your friends might say – they probably can't hear the music, anyway.

10. **Don't go** to any concert, play, movie, or other event unless you really want to go. (At your age, you have a laundry list of good excuses.)

11. Learn to use "You'll see" as a way to win an argument with any person younger than you. Anytime some punk argues a point with you, just chuckle good-naturedly, wag your head, and say, "**You'll see.**"

12. **Be *enthusiastic*,**
even if people think you're uncool—
because they'll think you're equally uncool
if you're aloof or cynical.

13. **Be *generous*** with your stuff.
Once you're gone,
somebody else is going to get it, anyway.

14. **Be confident.**

Let your identity
depend more
on what's inside
than what's outside.

15. Don't hesitate to do or say anything you really want—or need—to say or do.

16. Let your character shine. It contributes more to attractiveness than a dozen face-lifts.

17. Old age is a great time for outrage.
Try to say or do at least one
outrageous thing a week.

18. Remember, the older you get,
the more important it is NOT to act your age.

19. Treat people older than you with respect—
the way you'll want
to be treated when you get there.

20. When you play golf, tennis,
or whatever your game is,
play like an old pro,
not an old man or old woman.

21. It's OK to bribe your grandchild with candy
to help you check out gas-x.com
without letting anyone else know
you still haven't figured out this whole Internet thing.

22. Go ahead and be proud that your favorite
American Idols are
Neil Sedaka and George Washington.

23. It's perfectly acceptable not to answer the phone if you can't *retract* the La-Z-Boy before the answering machine kicks on.

24. You have permission to make your kids feel guilty for not calling on your birthday or Christmas, even though you were out *gallivanting* with old friends (and we mean **old** friends) and weren't home, anyway.

25. At a certain age,
it's proper church etiquette
to say you heard the sermon if you were awake
at the beginning and the end.

26. Don't hesitate to say "I told you so"
to your kids—or anyone else too stubborn
to listen to your sage advice.

27. Drive as slowly as you want.
You'll get there when you get there.

28. Savor your food.
Eating should not be a timed event.

29. Read more.

30. **Walk slowly and really enjoy the beauty around you.**

31. Listen more.

32. Be real with people.

33. Share your wisdom.

34. Pass on traditions.

35. Have strong opinions – and voice them.

36. *Ask* for what you want.

37. *Spoil* your grandkids.
It's part of the job description.

38. *Make* a difference.

39. *Support* the cause you believe in,
not necessarily the ones the celebrities are touting.

40. Learn something new.

41. Ignore popular opinion (you've seen it be wrong many times before).

42. Appreciate what you have.

43. Appreciate where you have been.

SKY
DIVING

44. Take a *real* vacation, not a working vacation.

45. Throw *caution* to the wind.

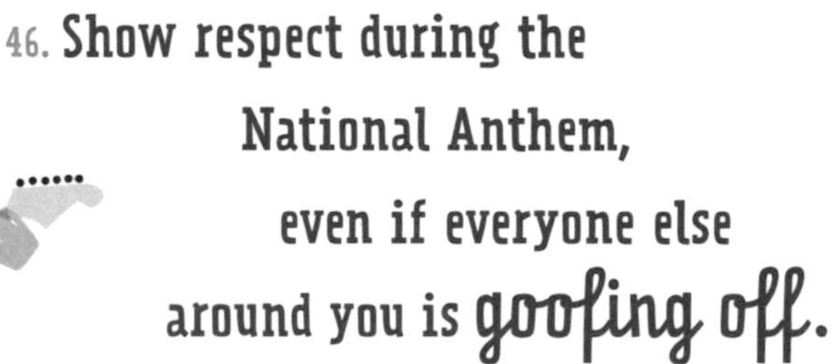

46. Show respect during the National Anthem, even if everyone else around you is *goofing off*.

47. Laugh out loud.

48. Never, ever be embarrassed.

49. Forget convention.

50. Always take the high road—
you know how to walk it.

How Old Is Old? *A Kid's-Eye View*

OLD!

They call us relics, fossils, fogies,
and geezers. But they also sit on our knees,
listen to our stories, give bear hugs,
and warm our hearts. Ever wonder
what kids really think about aging?
How old do you have to be before a
kid deems you officially ancient? Read on.
You might be surprised —
and you might even need a tissue.

My daddy is 40, and you can tell he's getting old because he's so tired all the time.

Brittany, age 5

I say you're not old if you can still eat regular food.

Curtis, age 10

My mom is 52, and she must not be old—because she can still whup me in tennis.

Austin, age 16

I think you're old at about 30
because that's when people start to look gross.

– Sergio, age 9

Ninety is old because it's almost 100.

Bryce, age 7

I guess 80 is old because that's when a lot of people die.

– Brennan, age 8

I think I'm getting old because I've lost
a lot of teeth this year.

– Alex, age 9

You're not old until you go to heaven –
and then you're new again.

– Ronnie, age 11

Fifty is, like, really old because that's almost a century!

– Andrea, age 6

I can't imagine living past 45 or so.
I think I'll be *so bored* by then.

Jenna, age 12

I can't say who is old
'cause that might hurt some old fogies' feelings and
they could have a *heart attack* or something.

Samantha, age 10

Fifty-five is old because
your eyesight starts to *go*. My mom is 55,
and she can't find anything anymore.

–Luiz, age 13

It's 50. At 40,
you're still pretty *well together*.
By 50, you're falling apart.

– Michael, age 12

I'd say 45—
you can't enjoy life anymore after that
because you're dying.

– Josh, age 13

No one is ever old until they're dead.

– Leroy, age 11

You're old when you turn 65
because that's when
you get wrinkly skin
and snow-white hair.

– Lily, age 9

You're not old till
you're more than 900.
Bible guys lived to be 900.

– Gabe, age 11

You're old as soon as you're born;
people say "two days old,"
or "three months old."

—James, age 12

Forty is old. Dude, after 40 your youth is gone.

– Brandon, age 14

You're old when you hit 80.
That's when you lose
your playful mind.

– Joe, age 14

Definitely 40.
That's when you start getting wrinkly.

– Darren, age 11

I'm gonna say 160.

Most people

don't live till then.

– Chris, age 8

You're old when you're 65 because that's when you get that "old people" smell.

– Elly, age 12

Old must be 100.
After that,
you can't
walk anymore.

– Christian, age 11

Forty is old because you have
your youth in your 20s,
your goals in your 30s,
but after 40, you just *kinda* give up.

– Katherine, age 15

You must get old at 45
because that's how old my dad is
and my mom is always calling him *"old man."*

– Taylor, age 11

I think you're old at about 70.
That's when you have to make
a grunting noise *every time*
you get up from a chair.

– Jay, age 14

Fifty is the official age for old,
because when he turned 50,
my dad started buying the *old people's* vitamins.

– Leslie, age 10

One hundred and five is old. (My grandpa is 104 and he's not old yet.)

—Jon, age 13

We'd love to hear
what you think of this book.
Please send your comments to:

book feedback
2501 mcgee, kansas city, missouri 64141-6580
or e-mail us at
booknotes@hallmark.com.